Parenting Boys

Parents and Children Describe What Works

(What Every Parent Should Know About Controlling a Child's Use of Technology)

Jose Doyle

Published by Rob Miles

© **Jose Doyle**

All Rights Reserved

Parenting Boys: Parents and Children Describe What Works (What Every Parent Should Know About Controlling a Child's Use of Technology)

ISBN 978-1-990084-29-4

All rights reserved. No part of this guide may be reproduced in any form without permission in writing from the publisher except in the case of brief quotations embodied in critical articles or reviews.

Legal & Disclaimer

The information contained in this book is not designed to replace or take the place of any form of medicine or professional medical advice. The information in this book has been provided for educational and entertainment purposes only.

The information contained in this book has been compiled from sources deemed reliable, and it is accurate to the best of the Author's knowledge; however, the Author cannot guarantee its accuracy and validity and cannot be held liable for any errors or omissions. Changes are periodically made to this book. You must consult your doctor or get professional medical advice before using any of the suggested remedies, techniques, or information in this book.

Upon using the information contained in this book, you agree to hold harmless the Author from and against any damages, costs, and expenses, including any legal fees potentially resulting from the application of any of the information provided by this guide. This disclaimer applies to any damages or injury caused by the use and application, whether directly or indirectly, of any advice or information presented, whether for breach of contract, tort, negligence, personal injury, criminal intent, or under any other cause of action.

You agree to accept all risks of using the information presented inside this book.

You need to consult a professional medical practitioner in order to ensure you are both able and healthy enough to participate in this program.

Table of Contents

INTRODUCTION 1

CHAPTER 1: GOOD PARENTING AS DEFINED BY ZEN 5

CHAPTER 2: HOW TO MANAGE DYSLEXIA 15

CHAPTER 3: ABOUT TODDLERS 25

CHAPTER 4: FINDING THEIR PERSONALITY 34

CHAPTER 5: HOW TO KEEP TECH SAVVY KIDS BUSY 38

CHAPTER 6: THE AMAZING PARENT; THE AMAZING BANK TECHNIQUE 42

CHAPTER 7: AVOIDING SIX PARENTING MISTAKES 50

CHAPTER 8: INTO THE WORLD OF A YOUNG CHILD 54

CHAPTER 9: YOUR CHILD IGNORES YOU COMPLETELY, TALKS BACK, OR EXPLODES (GIVEN A DIRECTIVE) 65

CHAPTER 10: LOVE, LIMITS, AND LETTING GO 83

- CHAPTER 11: VALUE OF DISCIPLINE AS AN EFFECTIVE PARENT 98
- CHAPTER 12: ACADEMICS AND SPORTS 107
- CHAPTER 13: 5 PRACTICAL TIPS TO MANAGING YOUR CHILD'S SCREEN TIME 116
- CHAPTER 14: WHY SIBLING RIVALRY HAPPENS: THE MAIN CAUSES 137
- CHAPTER 15: THE 11 COMMANDMENTS OF TODDLER DISCIPLINE 142
- CHAPTER 16: THE ABSENT PARENT – HOW TO DIFFUSE THE TENSION 154
- CHAPTER 17: PARENTING SKILLS 160
- CHAPTER 18: ON PARENT-CONNECTEDNESS AND ENTERING HIS WORLD 170
- CHAPTER 19: AWARENESS OF LOGICAL CONSEQUENCES 175
- CHAPTER 20: DON'TS OF BEING A CONSCIOUS PARENT 188
- CHAPTER 21: ENJOYING YOUR TEENAGERS 192

CONCLUSION.. **195**

Introduction

Many of us want to have children but many of us never stop to think how they will raise the kids when they have them. So when you get news that you are expecting a baby, what bothers you most is how you will take care of your unborn child. Well, this is really a natural process that doesn't require much; all you need to do is to go for checkups, observe your progress and any possible threats to the baby and anything else that would guarantee the safety of the baby. Everything goes on smoothly until the day you deliver your bundle of joy when it hits you that you are actually a parent.

For many new parents, the news come with mixed feelings; you feel as if you might not be a good parent and start feeling scared that you might not raise your kids to be as good as you've always pictured it in your mind. The wave of emotions could actually make you to get depressed. You feel you might make the mistakes that you've seen other parents make or feel that you really don't know anything that relates to raising an all rounded child who would become a responsible member of the society.

You feel that you might not do it right even when you don't know what that right is. The truth is that you won't hear many parents talking much about how to raise children well; they only point fingers when they see something wrong. In simple terms, you are all alone; it is just unfortunate that your child didn't come with a manual. You alone can design that blueprint for him or her to follow. And as the old saying goes, if you don't have a plan of where you are going, any road will take you there!

Well, if you are in a dilemma of what you should do to raise your child, here is some help. The truth is that raising kids in the right way can be the hardest job especially for first time parents especially because most first time parents do not know the dos and the don'ts of a parent and they sometimes find themselves overstepping or under stepping when it comes to raising up their kids. Parents may ignore some things that are really essential while raising kids and hence they may end up regretting how they raised their kids for the rest of their lives or they may even end up referring to themselves as bad parents depending on how their kids turned out in life.

This book will shed light on how to raise your kids right. Let it shine all the light you need to walk in the dimly lit path of parenting, which is filled with potholes.

To start from the beginning, we will start with raising infants and toddlers in the right way then move on with the parenting journey until your child is ready to leave your house i.e. teenage years.

Chapter 1: Good Parenting As Defined By Zen

We have formed a mindset as parents of how our children should behave and the person they should turn out to be in the society. Lest we forget, our children are humans who make mistakes just like we do. Actually, their mistakes are real as they are made out of total innocence.

Zen only accepts one kind of parenting whereby as a parent you have to make yourself less attached to results of your child's indiscipline and more mindful of the circumstances in your child's life that led them to it. By using this approach, you will have to invest largely on your emotions and have one on one moments with your child so as to understand them better. You have to see your child not as you want him or her to be but as a unique individual struggling to adapt to the ways of the world.

Many parents still believe in spanking as an effective way to punish. In Zen Habits, yelling and punishment does not go well with discipline and responsibility, but rather keeping calmness in every situation is the ultimate solution to a sense of discipline.

We sure are ready to start applying the Zen Habits as our parenting guide but first let's brainstorm on why your child might show signs of disobedience, refuse responsibility and the message it reflects:

Why Do Children Disobey?

To seek attention

Children are drawn to the way people treat them and so they like to be noticed by those who are around them especially their parents. In order to do so, the child may do something admirable which in most cases when it does not lead to the expected results, they turn to do the opposite, which is doing the wrong things. For instance, they may refuse to go to school in the morning with no reason so that you may pay attention to them.

To seek revenge

When a child feels like they have not been treated fairly by their parents or siblings, they start being rebellious towards that person. In such a scenario, they will for instance refuse to do any household chores, and even refuse to take a meal. Your child believes that by doing so, they are also hurting you.

Inferiority complex

Crazy as it may seem, children also like to feel that they are powerful and are able to take control of situations even those, which are beyond them. If you deny your child an opportunity to take control of certain situations they think they can take control of, he or she ends up acting up by engaging in indiscipline cases. For instance, they may want to change a blown up bulb in their room but when their older sibling is given that responsibility, they may end up taking the new bulbs and break them so that their sibling may not perform that duty.

Need for compassion

When a child is facing emotional distraught, the need for being shown love and affection becomes high. Since a child has not yet mastered the right channels of communication, they usually use their actions to seek for understanding. In this situation when you as a parent has not figured out that, avoiding them by showing you are too busy will result to chaos on their part, as they will feel neglected.

Lack of role models

Every child should grow up around people whom he or she can emulate. If a child grows up in a family whereby the policy is every man for himself and there is no family support, or where older family members lack discipline through such things like fighting each other, use of abusive language and engaging in drinking and smoking, the children will definitely have bad behavior too because no one will be there to guide them in the right path.

Parents' inconsistency

Children have to be subjected to straightforward ways of doing things.

When as a parent you say no to something today and tomorrow you say yes to the same thing, this will confuse your child and he or she will have a hard time showing discipline and taking charge of their responsibilities. This is the outmost reason why your child may disobey as they will resort to doing things in their own ways in which they deem fit. Consistency applies with all the above reasons as you should show it in your giving of attention, showing compassion, being a good role model, and so forth. Being unpredictable in any of these aspects of life could be what is making your children rebellious. Teach what you can comfortably sustain/live with for the rest of your life.

Having an insight of reasons your child may disobey brings us to the next sub topic on what to consider before putting into effect the Zen Habits technique of mindful discipline.

What to Consider when Giving Responsibility and Instilling Discipline

In light of being mindful parents, you should be mindful of these three things in order to discipline effectively.

Age

It is much easier to discipline children who are between ages 5-10 than dealing with teenagers. When your child becomes a teenager, they feel that they are more in control of their lives and would not want to be told what to do. This shows that discipline has to be incorporated in your child's life when they are still young so as to not depart from it. It is important to consider the age of your child as age bears different understanding for your child. A child of five years may not understand why you are punishing them when they do something wrong because for him or her differentiating between good or bad still does not make any sense. However, when dealing with a teenager, they do understand all the wrongs and consequences associated with them. When setting discipline strategies, "time-out" may go well with a child but for a teenager, it will backfire.

Health conditions

Children may have various health conditions that deter them from making wise decisions. For instance, there are those who have special needs such as Autism and ADHD. As much as it is required to put firm structures and guidance on every child, whether young or older, you cannot treat a special needs child in the same manner as others. With them, you have to be more patient and remind them of what is expected of them on a daily basis so that they may grasp before punishing them for the mistakes they do. Nevertheless, do not use their condition as an excuse for evading their punishment.

Wrong committed

It does not mean that some wrongs are more appropriate than others; what is looked into is the impact of the wrong committed. A child should know that there are consequences for every wrong that they commit. For instance, when a child lacks respect for their friends, teachers and parents, it becomes serious as without respect for others, the world will be a cruel place for your child. This should be taken into great concern than when your child for instance, refuses to brush their teeth. That will be the sure way of helping them become better.

Finally, it's time to look at Zen parenting techniques in our next chapter. Luckily, these are practical methods that you can apply right away.

Chapter 2: How To Manage Dyslexia

Whatever the origins of this condition, the fact remains that adults and children with dyslexia learn differently. If the difference is never accommodate within the specific education system, the student may have a difficulty in learning to write, spell and handle numbers. Some difficulties of this condition can be mild and no need for extra support, while other severe condition requires special treatment and specialist support. Early identifications and proper interventions are necessary in able people with dyslexia to achieve their full potentials and goals.

The assessment is not only for diagnose but also gives a great deal of information and tips about the learning profile of the individual. These information can be use in developing educational assessment plan will enable the teachers to identify appropriate teaching techniques which created for individual needs.

Studies shows that multi-sensory phases of learning are all beneficial. These are the means of many sensory channels that may be used in learning information.

☐Visual (diagrams, charts, colors)

☐Audio(hearing and listening comprehensively)

☐Kinesthetic (action and movement)

☐The more channels used the more effective the learning will be.

Technology is a big help for people with dyslexic. There is a wide range of technological aids available which can help people to manage their conditions.

Dyslexia is a long life condition. It will not go away. However, with the right support and aids, a dyslexic can still manage his condition to become self reliant, worker and good learner.

Ways or Helping Dyslexic Children to Succeed

Parents are the biggest foundation of support for dyslexic children. They hold on to parents who believed in their potentials and abilities. Here are some ways on how you can help your child to succeed and develop his/her full potentials.

Full Disclosure

Children want straight answer on what's happening to them. As their parent, educate yourself about their conditions and share them what you've learned about it. Through this, the child may be more are to his condition and able to figure out the things that surrounds him.

Strength Reinforcement

Dyslexic child spends a tremendous amount of time mastering writing and reading skills. When a child encounters learning challenges, it is associated with defeat and struggle. You must find a way on how your child will experience success. Be more attentive and aware,. Know the strength of your child and magnify these heads. Always remember that the child sees you as their whole so keep the overall worth. The child may not possessed skills and strengths in sports and other traditional phase but it can be more unique than what you expected.

Make reading fun and interesting

Dyslexic children may find reading too hard for them but the content will surely catch their interest. As their guardian, learn strategies on how you can make reading an interest of your child. You can use visuals or image about the story. It will increase the level of interest and motivation of the child.

Provide them role models

Show your child different personalities who succeed despite on dyslexia. Let them know that they have the same condition but they can be even more better than those. Providing role models for them will build an impact to their self confidence and motivations.

Providing Accommodations

Providing early interventions open the door for a great chance and opportunity for success in reading fluency. Keep in mind that maintaining the child's self-esteem intact is the most important factor in his/her survival in life or even in the classroom. Focus on what the child could learn in class and assist him/her to catch up on it well.

TIPS IN LEARNING TO WRITE AND READ

Always keep magazines and book on your child's room. They will even choose reading when they saw these books and magazines. Their curiosity will take them to learning.

Always bring a book wherever you and your child go.

Take time in reading story for him/her. This will relieve the boredom that your chili feels.

When you are cooking, let your child to instruct you by reading the recipes and instructions.

Whenever you are on the road, read road signs and different road maps.

Create a journal and encourage your child to do his/her own.

Be a model to your child in terms of reading and writing.

Encourage your child to the creativity of writing.

Provide him/her different instructional materials.

Join him/her while learning how to read and write

Social and Emotional Problems brought by Dyslexia

Dyslexia: Frustration and Discouragement

Dyslexic children often across failure in meeting expectations. Teachers and parents create a positive picture of dyslexic child as bright and enthusiastic even they have the difficulty in learning, reading and writing.

A dyslexic child tries very hard to meet the expectations of people surrounds him. And when time comes that he failed in this phase, he became frustrated and daunted. The pain brought by his failure is a achieved only by dyslexics difficulty to achieve and meet their goals. It is really true to those who develop sense of perfectionism in order for them to cope up with their worries. They tied up and grew up in the belief that it's terrible to make even a single mistake.

Their learning difficulty defines that they are capable of doing careless or stupid mistakes. It makes them feel worthless.

A dyslexic child frequently faces social relationships problems. These are the possible causes:

☐ They are physically and emotionally immature which lead to a poor social status.

☐ Their social immaturity can make them feel uncomfortable and disgusted in every situation.

☐ They have difficulties in reading social signs. They may be insensitive to the other people's sign and body language which will create distance and awkwardness.

☐ Dyslexia affects the speaking ability of the child. This may be a disadvantage when they became adults since it is one of the central images for having relationship with peers.

The difficulties brought by dyslexia can create serious challenge in child's life. Although everyone possessed strength and weakness, the dyslexic child is more exaggerated. Their strength can also be their weakness because these are closely related.

The world f dyslexic child is more challenging than the normal one. They need more support for survival and love for understanding. Just like other child they also ask for acceptance and care. They can't survive by their own that's why they need you as their parent. You should keep in mind whatever their condition has, still needs your unconditional love for him as your child. Consider him is a blessing and guide him to fully develop his own potentials that will help him to succeed and achieve his goals.

Chapter 3: About Toddlers

Ah, the wonder years. Your child is finally beginning to be self-sufficient. However, this is also a whole new territory, as your child is beginning to talk, learn and branch out with trying new things. You may find yourself wondering how you created a tiny Hitler. The truth is, this is a hard time for children, and a time where they are the most vulnerable of all.

Brain Development

As a child grows, their brain nearly doubles in size from the ages 1 to 5 years. Their brains are constantly taking in information and learning how to process everything they are taking in. This can lead to curiosity because as their brain grows, they want to learn more. You may find yourself faced with a child that is constantly getting into things that they shouldn't, and it feels like you can never blink. This is totally normal because children love to learn, and they want to learn about everything, even things they shouldn't be messing with.

You may also be faced with a child that asks "why" to every single thing. Most parents dread this phase. Along with the "why," there is also "what's this?" Both of these can leave a parent wanting to invest in ear plugs; however, as much as you wish you could stop it, you should entertain every question to the best of your ability. Children learn by asking questions. If you run out of answers, be honest with your child. You can say something along the lines of "I have run out of answers for this subject, do you have any other questions?" or "I am not sure, how about we change to a new subject?" You could even try looking up the answer with your child so that you are both learning.

It is also important to let your child experience the world around them. A lot of parents today are afraid to let their child get dirty for fear of germs. We will get to the germs part later, but here are some good reasons to let your child engage in sensory play. First off, it helps them develop their five senses, touch especially. They will learn to identify objects by feel. They will also learn to listen to the different sounds that things make, see how they look different. They will even learn, much to many parents dismay, how things taste. It is important that you make sure your child is not coming into contact with anything toxic because most of them will put things in their mouths.

STAY AWAY FROM SCREEN TIME! Technology has become a crutch for a lot of parents. They think that just because a game or television program is educational, they can use that to teach their children. Sometimes they help, but your child is only getting visual and auditory stimulation. They are not getting to touch things or smell them. They may learn their alphabet, but what good does that do when they do not know what order to read a book in? Screen time is causing children to be more delayed in their social skills as well because whenever a child is bored, they just have to ask for their tablet or other device to entertain them. Teach your children instead to do constructive things when they are bored, such as color or read a book. Teach them how to play by themselves with their toys, rather than expect to be entertained all the time. This helps the part of the brain that handles independence develop. You do not have to keep your child occupied all the time. They have to learn to be self-sufficient, as well as be guided by you. It is a fine balance that is hard to find.

Motor Skills

If this is your first child, chances are you are going to run to them every time they fall down. Every tear is cause for a band aid, even if there is no visible cut. The truth is, they are going to fall. They are going to get cuts and bruises, and they are going to cry. You are not doing them any favors by rushing to their aid for every little thing. It's understandable. You just want your child safe and happy, but just because they fall does not mean that you have to rush over to give them a ton of cuddles.

Studies have actually shown that this is detrimental to their development. They recognize your fear, and they feel that they too should be afraid of falling. When in reality, falling is just a way of life. Even adults trip and fall sometimes. Unless the child is genuinely hurt, here are some things that you should try instead of rushing over to them.

The first thing you should do is wait. Judge their reaction. If they do not start crying immediately, chances are they are fine. Encourage them. Tell them good job, and to get up and try again. If you are not scared and treat them as if falling is normal, they will not cry unless they get hurt. They will also be more willing to continue to get better, rather than regress and want to be carried more than they walk.

If your child does immediately cry, calmly walk over to him or her and look for any signs of injury. Be calm and reassuring. Tell your child how good they did, and that you can't wait to see them do it again. Children respond well to a calm reassuring parent, even if they have a minor scrape or bruise. If the injury is minor and there is no broken skin, give them a hug and tell them that it will be alright. If you want to kiss the injury, that is up to you, but generally, if you do not point it out, they will not even realize that it is there.

If there is broken skin and the child is bleeding, you still should remain calm. Asses the injury and see if it needs medical attention or if it simply needs cleaned and a band aid put on it. If it is a simple little cut that needs cleaned, the best step to take is to find a red washcloth. Children tend to get scared when they see blood because they do not understand it. Use a red washcloth to clean their injury and put a band aid on it. Once you do that, hug them and tell them that everything is okay and that they should try again.

If the injury needs medical attention, it is still not a time to panic. You do not want your child to be scared, and potentially hurt themselves more. Be calm, and cover any part that is bleeding with a red washcloth. Apply pressure to the wound, and then get them to the doctor swiftly. If your child asks what is going on, calmly tell them that they have an injury and that they have to see a doctor to make it better. If it is a bad injury, they will probably cry. Soothe them, and tell them that these things happen and that they will be okay. Children are surprisingly resilient.

The most important thing is to make sure that you never scare your child away from exploring things. You want them to learn how to walk, run, and jump. Occasionally, they will want to explore things that you don't want them touching, but that will be discussed in a later chapter on the foundations of parenting.

Chapter 4: Finding Their Personality

Toddlers often have already developed a personality of their own. However, most parents try to override their child's personality and creativity because they feel it does not run well with how their household runs. As a parent, you think you know what is best, and most of the time you do. However, you have to understand, that toddlers are becoming little people. They have their own ideas, and they are starting to think for themselves.

There are some tips that you can use to help find their personality. It is important that you remember, your child and their feelings are valid. They are not little robots for you to order around and treat like they are supposed to be zombies. Children need support from their parents to become their own person, and it starts when they are a toddler.

Of course, you want to make sure they are respectful, and a child with an attitude will need more discipline than a sweet and already respectful child; however, you do not want to disregard your toddler's attitude if they have one. This is because one day, they can become a persuasive leader and very passionate. Put them on the right track to become a good leader. Do not try to squash their can do attitude.

Listen to Them

Your child may not be the most articulate yet, but they still want you to listen to them when they talk. Children have the craziest ideas, and listening to those ideas can give you valuable insight to how their minds work. If your child is talking about something that you find impossible, don't say that. Listen to what they are saying. Let them know that it has not happened yet and that they should work on making it happen. Build them up, and don't tear them down. Even if you don't understand a word they are saying, listen to the passion in their voice. Children are the most passionate people on the planet. They have not yet hit society where passion is seen as being crazy, so it is shushed. Don't stunt their passion.

Believe in Them

Children are very impressionable. You could have a toddler that is very outspoken and ambitious that turns into a slacker as they get older. This is because someone along the way told them that they were not good enough, or that what they wanted couldn't be done. Most of the time, sadly, this is their parents. From the time they are toddlers, you should believe in them. Let them climb that rock, but just be there to catch them. Let them try to read, and help them. Be there to raise them up, and help them reach their potential. Even if you are skeptical, tell your child it is possible.

Your child will develop their personality more in their toddler years, than all their years together after that. You want to give them the right start.

Chapter 5: How To Keep Tech Savvy Kids Busy

At these modern times, most of the kids are now considered technologically inclined or tech-savvy. It is normal to see kids playing with the computers, laptops, cell phones, game consoles, and play stations. Parents of these tech-savvy kids should know how to keep their children interested; otherwise, their kids won't be able to listen to them.

There are various ways to keep tech-savvy kids occupied and safe at the same time. Here are some tips:

Use of Cell Phones

Children who are technically inclined would love to hold their cell phones instead of their books or crayons or pencils more. They may not be chatting or texting on their phones yet but they would surely be interested to play games with it. And the good thing is there are applications that can be downloaded to your kid's phone for their enjoyment. It is better if they can listen to the sound and music while they play.

Here are a few suggested applications ready for download free:

- Paint: Kids would love to play with colors and experiment while matching and combining colors. Paint is a good application where kids can draw whatever they want to draw and color it with whatever color they like.

- Scribble-Lite: A fun sophisticated etch-a-sketch drawing application.

- Smack-talk: An application where a child can speak to a microphone and an animal will imitate or repeat what he said. Toes and pitches can be adjusted.

IPod

IPod downloadable applications include the StoryNory. Although the stories have remained the same, the story-telling technology has advanced so much in a span of a few years. Parents can now download these applications so that kids can listen to some interesting stories they would love to hear using technology. So when the little bookworm becomes bored, just tell him to tune in to his IPod and he can listen to the stories for hours. It will be more interesting if he uses a cool headset.

Computer

Kids do know how to manipulate a laptop. To keep them occupied, download games such as plants vs. zombies, Hangaroo, hide and seek, or typing-speed test. They would surely love these games and won't be a nuisance – at least for a while.

Chapter 6: The Amazing Parent; The Amazing Bank Technique

You have that amazing life without kids now. Yes, that is true but there is no how you wouldn't encounter children. I did meet a woman and she told me while smiling; I love children, but it is not possible for me to eat a whole one. I smiled back.

The mistake we keep making that seems to be the biggest in our parenting life is placing substantial value on the pursuit of money to make our children happy. Money is good. Getting money is important, making money is nice but not at the expense of the attention you need to give to your child. Nowadays, parents work long hours and the children suffer for it. You should never put money before your child. That amazing relationship comes from an amazing life of healthy relationship you have with your child.

You may have this book in your hands because you are struggling to work out that love relationship between you and your child or how to guide him or her. All struggles would end when you become an amazing parent. While you are absorbing the words here, you may come across few myths about parenting. But the most important things are the techniques and principles which I would want you to grasp firmly. So that you'll understand them anytime they are completely lost.

Every day I go to work. I meet parents all the time. Most of them are concerned mothers who would explain to me in great detail what they really feel or think is wrong with their children. What follows next is always surprising. Would you like to talk to her so you can see if you can fix it. What they expect me to do is to talk to the child and when he or she walks out from my office he/she becomes different because I have been able to fix the child.

Obviously the children are not toys or machines that need fixing. When parents meet me their expectation is that the child wouldn't be the same as before and everything would just stop instantly. Like I have a magic wand or something. I can show you how to fix children but you'll end up with information what may be completely useless to you.

The first process in being an amazing parent is understanding that it is not all about the child but about the parent. So the first thing I do when I am asked to fix a child. I sit back, remember all the training over all the years and then that little dog whispers to me. Get the parent in and talk to them. When you get a dog, you as the dog owner would still have to retrain that dog. Parents need to be retrained just like their kids. Most parents haven't been on training programs on how to raise a child. They just jump into it and mess everything up.

I would provide you some examples here. These examples include children from age 8 upwards. So you have the age bracket to be 8 to 15. What I do first is that I start with the story of the trusted bank building. I would let the little children understand that no matter what they want in life, which may come right now, at the weekend or next year, thee parents alone would say yes of give them access to such benefits if they have enough good attitude in the bank. If their currency is yes.

Furthermore, becoming an amazing parent involves the Amazing Bank Technique.

What is this technique? This is a very simple technique. We all know that children need a perfect blend of discipline and praise right? I use 90% praise so we have a ratio of 90:10. Praise is easy and it works 100% more for the child. Parents don't understand this. It is sad that I have never met a parent who uses praise like I do. What he/she does is to point out the errors in the child's behavior. While they are busy pointing errors the child sees the errors as a regular parlance. Understanding this trick is the first process in becoming a parent.

When I meet a child, I understand the child within possible seconds and minutes. What I do is I set up my understanding by knowing what goes around the house. What they can do or what they do at home. I ask them about jobs and chores. Indirectly, I am teaching the child to contribute to family and the household. I make this as practical as possible because I would take them home and once the chores are done I would let the child know that he/she is adding currency into his/her bank. The currency only comes when they take part in extra jobs. This propels the child to do more.

Okay, this is all theory. Let's get practical. This is how it works.

I once met a 14 year old girl who wasn't interested in the amazing bank technique. She wanted to pull out of the plan even before it started. I got her back in when I said, "I'm the only person on earth who can get your parents off your back" This sounded cool and really arrested her attention. That was the icebreaker. I started explaining to her how she would reestablish that position vacant in her family.

This girl had a history of running out of school, not doing her homework leading to bad grades and making bad language are regular dialect. I took my time to listen to her. Something her parents never did. Because the only attention she got was that of hostility. She was motivated to do the right thing, to store good attitude in her bank.

Fast forward to the next two weeks. She arrived with her mother and the mother was; she has become a totally different person, she is now nice to her brother and sister, she does her homework, never leaves school and does her chores. The mother is excited but when the child walks in after. She is sad.

"With all I have done, they still don't recognize me or say something nice"

This is very typical of parents. We don't recognize the effort of our children. Even when we do, we fail to give praise let alone see the time the child needs praise. The later part of the day was spent with the mother explaining to her the idea of her daughter building a bank of good attitude. A place were the currency is good jobs in exchange for special treats. It was easy for the mother to adjust to this and she began to praise her child more. And they lived happily ever after.

Chapter 7: Avoiding Six Parenting Mistakes

As parents, we are humans, there is every tendency that we would make mistakes. In fact, this book is full with a lot of mistakes right now. But there are still some common mistakes parents make. We should try as much as we could to avoid such mistakes. Here are six parenting mistakes to avoid:

Being Inconsistent

When it comes to toddlers parenting, do your best to continue in what you might have started. Don't relent. Show your child the consequences of his actions whenever he does wrong. Don't be too tired to do the right thing. The more consistent you are, the more predictable things become, and children learn through rote learning. When it keeps repeating itself, it sticks.

Overdoing Family Time

Spending time with the whole family is fun, but some parents just go to the extreme. Maybe because of over zealousness and happiness. Clinical psychologist Thomas Phelan, author of 1-2-3 Magic says, "Kids cherish time alone with one parent." He point out, "One-one-one time is fun for parent too, because there is no sibling rivalry to contend with."

Offering too much help

Sometimes, children need to figure out things by themselves. Some parents jump into helping them whenever they are faced with trouble. No! Leave them, let them enjoy their liberty. Besty Brown Braun, author of you're Not the Boss of Me, says. "parents who offer too much help may be sabotaging their young children's ability to become self-reliant,"

Talking too much

Phelan, a pediatric psychologist says "Talking can lead to what I call the talk-persuade-argue-yell-hit pattern" as a parent, you don't talk too much. You give short explanations. Don't explain everything, sometimes leave them in the dark, they would figure it out.

Serving only Kiddie Food

Braun says "Children love the fight over food. If we make a fuss about it, it becomes a much bigger deal than it needs to be." Braun's point of view is that, as long as there is something to eat, you don't need to worry. Well, variety, they say is the spice of life. Make sure your toddler is fed with a steady diet of nutritionally irresistible food.

Getting Rid of the Crib

Altmann, a child psychologist says, "Some moms wear themselves out because they have to lie down with their child every night, they don't realize they're the ones who set the pattern." What do cribs do? They promote good sleep habits for the child and the child alone, not you. When a child reaches a height of 35 inches, you should allow him climb out of his crib. It is fun.

Chapter 8: Into The World Of A Young Child

Having reiterated that raising your children require good parenting paired with good disciplining and parental power, it is now time to deliberately break down the things you need to do to raise your children right. Now, there are several things you need to do to accomplish this task and it all depends on the stage where your child is at.

From the age of 3 to 12, your kid is considered a young child. This stage of growth is the most crucial time to discipline your child because this is considered their formative years. This is the time where they get to know the world more, how it works and its ways. This is when you distinguish what is good from bad, what is right from wrong. This is the right time to teach them about life, explaining it to them in the simplest way to level it to their own understandings.

However, the main hindrance to actually doing this task well is the lack of time and patience of the parents in properly disciplining their children. Balancing work and home duties are always a struggle for mothers and fathers. The stress of simultaneously juggling childrearing and work-related responsibilities take a toll on numerous parents' personal and professional lives.

While managing a career and a household leaves some parents delusional and drained, others seem to be able to easily balance parenting with their full-time works. It is proven by psychological studies that parents who are able to raise well-adjusted children while also maintaining a professional career are the most fulfilled. And the secret to this success is to start training and disciplining your kids at a young age.

The key to good disciplining is putting responsibilities to your kid, little by little as they grow up. This will train them into handling the future responsibilities that life will throw at them. Children who value responsibility and actually act on it at an early stage, shows higher success rate in the professional field. This is because they lean the value of work at an early age.

A lot of parents think that when their children is busy with music recitals and soccer games, the value of work imparted on them is enough. Yes, there is a certain drive and responsibility that your children learn when they strive for something they want to achieve. However, that is not enough. These pursuits of leisure are disciplines of a different kind that have little to do with the basic responsibility to the family.

Teaching your children the value of teamwork in the house will surely help your household by a mile. A typical family will function with the help of all its members. That's how it works. Everyone depends on the contribution of everyone else. This includes your children helping you out with household chores. This will be the first responsibility they will be given in their lives and you should teach them how important this is. Not only because you just want to get things done, but you should emphasize that instilling the value of work and responsibility at an early age will benefit them greatly when they grow up.

A great tip to do this is by dividing your household chores into two categories: routine contributions and extra jobs. The routine chores of your children such as making beds, sweeping the floor, washing the dishes and dusting the furniture, should be part of their unpaid responsibilities. The extra chores such as bathing the dogs, washing the car and watering the garden, should provide incentives for the children.

As a parent, you need to clearly distinguish the two and impose them properly. They need to know why they need to do their routine jobs every day. Make them understand that assigning a chore means giving them the responsibility to do it and if they don't do it nobody else would. They need to know that this is their contribution to make the household up and running.

Household chores are the responsibility of your children but good parenting requires proper motivation in order to make it less of a burden for your kids. This is where the extra jobs come in. Allow them to gain something from their hard-work. An incentive would be great like money or an ice cream treat. Little things that will inspire your kids to do extra chores in the house. This will teach them that in the future, when they have proper and stable jobs, they get rewarded for their hard work.

It is also important that as a parent, you do hands-on instructions to your kid when it comes to their chores. Do not expect, especially when your child is still young and adapts fairly slow compared to adolescents, that they can get it in one instruction and in one try. Children learn best by conscious imitation. Instead of saying "Go and clean your room," do the task with your child. Show him or her how to properly make the bed, how to tidy up the closet and how to arrange the dresser. Using this trick will help your child get the chore done easier and would retain it better.

Another great tip regarding household chores and work in general is to always make it a fun time for your kids. It is your responsibility as a parent to constantly make chores as pleasant as possible. Imagine, if you keep on nagging about unfinished and undone chores, your child will build up a negative attitude towards work. Be with them when they are working and tell funny stories to make it enjoyable. Do not forget to compliment them when they do a good job because this will also serve as a motivation for them to always do well in their chores.

However, not all jobs are always easy and fun. There will be times wherein your child will feel lazy and think of clever excuses to avoid doing the chores he or she needs to be doing. And as a parent, you need to be firm and consistent that your child needs to do it no matter what. Never fall into the trap of doing your child's chore because the moment you do, your child will keep on repeating it with several other wise excuses causing more problems in your plate.

Also, do not expect precision from your child in every little thing that he or she does. Some children do not have the coordination to properly make a bed or sweep the floor, at a certain age of course. However, say for example your child is already 10 years old and does a sloppy job at folding his or her shirts that argument will greatly differ. Do not ignore it and constantly teach him or her how to properly do it. Always check and inspect his or her closet if it is neatly piled.

It is important to require what is best from your child's capability at their certain age. This is a good training for them, especially when you want to make them responsible inside and outside the house. Do not tolerate sloppiness because this is a hard habit to break once they get accustomed to it. Teachers and future bosses have little tolerance from it compared to parents so make sure you train them well.

Though children can easily be discouraged when they get assigned to a chore that they are not capable of, at their certain age. If they constantly get reminders from you to do it well but can't seem to deliver, it saddens them and makes them hate the chore itself. Now as a parent, it is your job to determine whether or not your kid is capable of a certain chore you assign to him or her.

A good place to begin with is tidying up with toddlers. At the age of 2 or 3, you can teach your child to keep his or her own toys after playing. At the age of 4 or 5, you can start teaching them to throw their garbage in the trash can or picking up tiny trashes around the house when they see one and so on and so forth. Washing the dishes and sweeping the floor can come later when your child is about 10 years old and has a fair amount of coordination. You can increase the difficulty of the chore as your child grows older.

Also, make sure that your child finishes the chore he or she is assigned to. Completion of a task is a very important skill your child needs to learn and value. Occasionally, your child will likely say he or she finished the job. Do not forget to check and see if it passes your standards and do not hesitate to call him or her back if it does not.

Teaching your children the value of work and responsibility is no easy task. It requires constant supervision from you and a lot of time. However, your hard work will surely pay off in the future life of your child and that will always be worth it.

Chapter 9: Your Child Ignores You Completely, Talks Back, Or Explodes (Given A Directive)

Why you B*tch: There is no confirmation that your child heard you (ignoring you), the talking back is exhausting and the explosive tantrums are a safety concern (to themselves/others), embarrassing in public and/or time consuming to de-escalate from.

Parent: Go brush your teeth Lizzie, time for bed.

Child: Silence.

Parent: Lizzie, I said go brush your teeth.

Child: Silence. Stares at floor.

Parent: Did you hear me? Get in there and brush your teeth now please!

Child: Silence.

Why the problem exists: Somewhere along the way, your child has learned that these three ways of responding to a directive are acceptable. Consider where they may have learned this. How do you respond to directives from other adults/your child? What tone or behaviors does your child exhibit as coping skills when being redirected?

How to start Parenting: Consider the following to identify which response your child generally gives when redirected or given a directive: You start parenting by re-teaching them how you expect them to act when given a prompt. This re-teaching method will vary between the three groups.

The 'Shy' Child (Ignores You)

Parents who have a child who shuts down or is unresponsive to directives will often say that their child is shy. If so, please see Chapter One again, making excuses, read it three more times, then rejoin the group when finished.

A child who displays the personality of being shy (limited conversation or input on initial meetings, quiet or timid gestures around non-family members) is not to be confused with the child who uses shyness as a coping skill for bad behavior. The difference? If the child only displays these gestures when given directives, rest assured they're using it as a means to avoid consequences.

Quiz yourself: Your child is running around the library, playing tag with random children and pulling books off the shelf and using them as Frisbees. As their voice carries across the room you notice you're getting annoyed glances and say, "Brandon, enough, put those books back and come stand next to me." Suddenly the child is timid and looks at the books with disinterest. They may stand perfectly still, turn their back slightly, or gaze at the floor. Do you have a shy child or are they ignoring you?

Answer: Ignoring you.

What to do? Teach them an appropriate response to use for when they are given a directive. It will establish they have heard and understood you so you can move on to bigger directives.

Parent: "Brandon, put those books back and come stand next to me."

Child: Silence.

Parent: "Brandon, you need to put those books back before I'll get you this book, if you understand say 'Yes Mommy'."

Child: "Yes Mommy."

Parent: "Great, I'm glad you heard me. Put those books away so we can leave, okay?"

Child: "Yes Mommy."

I remember the look of astonishment when I coached a parent to employ this tactic. It was instantaneous and triggered a response from an otherwise tight lipped child (under the circumstances). By setting the child up for success, I directed the parent to establish why and how the child should respond. By gaining an understanding that the child heard the parent, it opened the door for the parent to request that the directive be followed.

The Lawyer Child (Talks Back)

Children should legally be allowed to practice as lawyers. Their naturally naive perception of the world makes them the crème de la crème of their arguments: they genuinely believe that their opinion, regardless of logistics, is the right one. As a human this trait is imperative to allow the human mind to expand and learn. As parents this trait drives us bat shit crazy when all you want your child to do is put the bowl of milk into the sink before the school bus gets there, not explain why the milk can't be flushed or dumped into the Hess truck or given to FeFe.

Why you B*tch: Sometime around the age of four the one worded response of "Why" creeps its way into the vocabulary of your child. When you give a directive, your child somehow simultaneously taps into the limitless supply of "why's" that can counteract your request. What you are left with is a twenty-minute tangent of discussion (argument, explanation, explosion...I digress) that leaves you utterly clueless as to what the request was in the first place. In other words: Child-1, Parent-0.

Why the problem exists: Over explanations and giving your child ammo to begin with. Consider the two scenarios below.

Child: "Mom, can I have a cookie before dinner?"

Parent: "No I want you to eat your whole meal."

Child: "I'm really hungry."

Parent: "Have an applesauce. Dinner will be ready soon."

Child: "I don't want an applesauce, can't I just have one cookie?"

Parent: "I said no, wait until after dinner."

Child: "So I can have a cookie after dinner?"

Parent: "Yes."

Child: "Can I have two cookies?"

Now watch as that situation is internalized and used as ammo for the following night.

Parent: "What are you doing put that applesauce back."

Child: "But I can have it."

Parent: "Dinner is soon, I didn't give permission to have it. Put it back."

Child: "You told me yesterday I could have it. I didn't ask for a cookie I just want the applesauce."

Parent: "That was yesterday."

Child: "I'm so hungry Mom, applesauce is better than a cookie. You said I could have it yesterday and I will eat my whole meal, I promise."

Parent: "I said no, please put it back."

Child: "That's not fair, why could I have it yesterday?"

That's where you get pinned. You're stuck between something you tried to bargain a day earlier and the realities of what is happening right before you. You've lost before you even had a chance to realize what was happening.

How to start Parenting: Short. Concise. Sentences. Without any additional fillers, explanations or clauses that can be used against you. Consider the same above conversation.

Child: "Mom, can I have a cookie before dinner?"

Parent: "No, thanks for asking, dinner is soon."

Child: "I'm really hungry."

Parent: "Great, dinner will be ready soon."

Child: "But mom, why can't I have one."

Parent: "I answered that already, you tell me."

Child: "Because dinner is soon?"

Parent: "Yes."

Child: "Can I have a cookie after dinner?"

Parent: "When do you always have dessert?"

Child: "After dinner."

Same conversation, less leverage the child is able to use against the parent later. While it is important to explain the "why's" to children, parents have a hard time knowing when to stop explaining. Repeating or reiterating the same explanation two to three times in most cases is sufficient to drive your point across. After that, you need to put the ball in the child's court and ask them to tell YOU the reason why.

This is important for two reasons. It allows the child to pause, seriously consider the reason, then state it back to you so you know they heard you and understood.

Second, it allows them to say no to themselves.

Child: "But mom, why can't I have one."

Parent: "I answered that already, you tell me."

Child: "Because dinner is soon?"

Parent: "Yes."

The child had to come to the conclusion that the reason a cookie was not allowed was because of dinner being soon. You didn't have to tell them a third time, or listen to them whine four or five more times about the same question. Just as a child will try and break down your walls by asking the same question over and over, you can reverse that strategy and ask THEM why they think the answer is no. That game gets old pretty quick, and they are more satisfied with being turned down because technically they came to that conclusion themselves.

Wiley Coyote Child (Explodes)

Road Runner from the Wile E. Coyote cartoon was a genius. Wile E. Coyote's was on a desperate mission to capture the Road Runner. Wile would build elaborate traps to capture him, and just when you thought the coyote was successful Road Runner would 'Beep Beep' away into a cloud of dust leaving the coyote standing in a cloak of explosive debris.

As parents that same cloud of debris lingers over our heads in the form of a child's tantrum. Sometimes it's expected and calculated (no nap, stayed up late, hungry, and in the middle of a grocery store) and sometimes it comes out of left field in the middle of your family's get together. Before your child reaches the brink of a disastrous melt down in aisle nine, read on.

Why You B*tch: An explosive child reacts aggressively, loudly or verbally inappropriately. Flying objects, sibling slapping and potty mouth are common reactions. An explosive child can be dangerous, embarrassing, and hard to manage.

Why the problem exists: First, breathe parent, you are (slightly) not to blame. In the nature vs. nurture argument children have an innate tendency to be aggressive, which makes sense. These innate reactions to stimuli are what allowed the human race to overcome and flourish as a species. At the same token, aggression that is not controlled or channeled to other outlets can lead to an adolescent with heavier behavioral problems later in life such as drug abuse and violent crime.

So what gives? Coping skills. Your little ticking time bomb lacks, severely misinterprets or otherwise has no use for any coping skills. You're about to change that.

How to start Parenting: Focus on the behavior, not the cause of the aggression or explosion. Consider the family of three I worked closely with for several years. Their son Jeremy, age 9, would lash out physically to his siblings or friends at school if (while playing any competitive type game) he lost. While feelings of defeat or "sore loser" type behaviors are commonplace, this child would physically attack, throw objects at the "winner" and have a melt down of epic proportions including foul language and death threats. He was the perfect example of an explosive child.

I challenge you to reward this type of child. I know, I know. You want to reach through your smart device and strangle me, just hear me out. If there is one positive attribute about an explosive child it's that they are generally over willing and enthusiastic; this is why their reactions are so grandeur. Coping skills 101 teaches us to provide an alternative outlet (high five instead of hit), redirect the negative behavior (secret handshake, winners dance, etc.) and REWARD the positive.

Jeremy's situation called for the following solution: High five the winner, do a secret handshake (they made up), and re-challenge the victor to another game. If another game ensued/no melt down happened then a token was added to a chart on the family refrigerator; Jeremy added the token to the chart himself. If any negative reactions ensued, a token was taken away from the chart on the refrigerator (this too was done by Jeremy only). When the chart was full Jeremy got to pick out another game to share with his friends or siblings (video game, board game, etc.). If the tokens disappeared from the chart completely THEN games were put in 'time out' in a closet until Jeremy earned tokens back by doing household chores.

It took approximately six weeks for Jeremy to take control over his own emotions and consistently overcome his aggression when facing a loss in a game or otherwise. The reason being that the rewards far outweighed the punishments and his lack of coping skills was channeled in a positive way. Giving a child the CHOICE and direction to act out appropriately is sometimes all it takes. We are not born to know how to react in times of loss, defeat or frustration; it is our job as parents to provide them with appropriate coping skills to challenge their innate tendencies and to comply with social standards.

TIP: The expectations of alterative outlets and redirection of behaviors MUST be established when the child is in a calm state and BEFORE such explosions. Trying to navigate an emotionally distraught child with new skills in the midst of a melt down is equivalent to trying to breathe underwater. They need to know what is expected of them when they can listen, understand and ask questions at their leisure.

Chapter 10: Love, Limits, And Letting Go

The preeminent pediatrician Benjamin Spock once described the key to raising happy and emotionally healthy children as the Three L's: love, limits, and letting go. While many writers have emphasized either love or limits, research and experience have shown that optimal parenting combines the two.

The psychologist Diana Baumrind bridged this gap in her work on parenting styles. She contrasted four major parenting styles, authoritarian, authoritative, permissive-indulgent, and permissive-uninvolved. These four parenting styles are defined by the levels of love and limits utilized by the parent.

Authoritarian parenting is high in limits but low in love and emphasizes firm control.

The authoritarian parent tends to set rigid rules, demand obedience, and use strategies such as the withdrawal of love or approval to force a child to conform. These parents are more likely to use physical punishment or verbal insults to elicit the desired behavior. They tend to lack warmth and may seem cold and distant to their child. Children with authoritarian parents may be well-behaved but are also likely to be moody and anxious, and tend to be followers rather than leaders.

Permissive-indulgent parenting is high in love but low in limits, the permissive-indulgent parent demonstrating abundant affection. This parent may be openly loving but sets few if any limits, sometimes even when the child's safety may be at risk. Permissive-indulgent parents make few demands for responsible behavior and there are often no real consequences for misbehavior. Children of permissive parents often have problems with controlling their impulses, often appear immature, and resist accepting responsibility.

Permissive-uninvolved parenting is low in both love and limits, which at its extreme begins to look like rejection and/or neglect. Children with uninvolved parents are likely to struggle in many areas of daily living, tend to do poorly in school, and, as they get older, are more likely to exhibit antisocial behavior and depression.

Authoritative parenting, which is high in both love and limits, is considered the ideal parenting style and seems to produce children with high levels of self-reliance and self-esteem who are socially responsible, independent and achievement-oriented, and show more individual initiative and social responsibility. Authoritative parents set clear expectations and have high standards. They monitor their children's behavior, use sensible and appropriate discipline, and encourage their children to make decisions and learn from their mistakes. They are also warm and nurturing, treating their children with kindness, respect and affection. Authoritative parents love their children unconditionally and set and enforce reasonable but consistent limits.

Decades of research support an authoritative parenting style as the best way to raise a happy and psychologically healthy child. Love your child unconditionally, express discontent and disapproval of their behaviors but not of them, set and impose reasonable but consistent limits.

Spoiling a child is never a good idea but indulging your child now and then is one of the joys of parenthood. I remember visiting friends in New England who bought lobsters for our celebratory dinner. Their five year-old son whined that he wanted my lobster instead of his despite the fact that they were fairly identical. The mother, who practiced a permissive-indulgent parenting style, embarrassedly asked me to give him my lobster, which I politely refused. After dinner, he asked his father for a can of tuna, to which the father responded, "You just had dinner and you won't eat the tuna". Two or three whines later, the father opened the can of tuna, at which point the child left the kitchen. Giving a young child lobster for dinner is indulging him (if he likes lobster), giving in to his whining and doing things against your better judgment (like asking me to give Jimmy my lobster) is spoiling.

Your Thanks for Doing it Right

Do you wonder why your child is an angel outside the home but far from an angel with you? It may well be because you've done your job right. This paradox makes sense if you take a developmental perspective.

The child's earliest experiences have great impact on the person she becomes, and the early bonds between parent and child have profound effect on this outcome. Freud wrote that so long as we trace development from its final outcome backwards, the chain of events appears continuous, and provides valuable insight.

Perhaps the most important thing to teach your baby is that he can depend on you unconditionally, can trust you unconditionally, that you will love and protect your baby unconditionally. This became dramatically apparent to Anna Freud while working with orphans in London shortly after World War II. Freud was puzzled by some children coming through the bombings unscathed while others appeared devastated. What Freud discovered that the children who someone with them to whom they were strongly attached and could trust unconditionally had survived emotionally intact while the children without an attachment figure experienced emotional ruin. When your child feels they can count on your unconditional love and support, they can survive bombs falling over their heads.

So why does this produce little monsters? For the answer we turn to the work of the psychologist Eric Erikson, who talked about the young child's need for autonomy and independence. According to Erikson, self-control and self-confidence begin to develop in early childhood as children strive to do more on their own. They have a strong drive to do for themselves and to control their destiny but, being young, have a very limited number of ways to exercise their need for power and control, so (as discussed earlier) they typically they oppose, defy, or otherwise torture the person with whom they feel most comfortable, knowing that, however challenging their behaviors, they will be safe and loved. Your thanks for doing such a great job is that you become the one with whom they can safely play out this need for power and control.

Erikson wrote that it is essential for parents not to be overprotective at this stage and to allow some degree of independence, that is, to begin the long and often painful process of letting them go. Erickson believed that a parent's level of protectiveness will influence the child's ability to achieve autonomy, which can produce feelings of shame as the child learns to doubt his or her abilities. Erikson believed that children who experience too much doubt at this stage will lack confidence in their powers later in life. Accordingly, you need to begin to let them go before you feel real comfortable doing so. Combined with unconditional love and reasonable, firm, and consistent limits, you have the best chance of achieving your goal of raising a happy and emotionally healthy child.

Play and Imagination

My first position in this field was in one of the first early intervention programs in New York City, where I worked with an occupational therapist (among other professionals). I thought of OTs as working in veteran's hospitals and couldn't imagine what OT had to do with two and three year-olds. When I asked the OT about this, she said the job of the OT is help the client perform their occupation, and the occupation of the child is to play. This has stuck with me all these years for its wisdom.

To play is to engage in activity for enjoyment and recreation rather than a practical purpose: it is about the process and not the product. It is child directed. Research indicates that children learn best in an environment which allows them to explore, discover, and play. Play enhances language development, social competence, creativity, imagination, and thinking skills and, as J. L. Frost has written, "play is the chief vehicle for the development of imagination and intelligence, language, social skills, and perceptual-motor abilities in infants and young children". The pioneering Russian psychologist Lev Vygotsky wrote that children engaged in play not only practice what they already know but also learn new things. Play not only reflects thoughts and ideas but also creates them.

Einstein wrote that imagination is far more important than knowledge, and child-directed imaginative play is a great way to promote cognitive/intellectual development. Identifying letters or colors is not intelligence, taking little pieces of plastic and giving them life and creating a story promotes intellectual development. The child far less interested in the electronic toy than the box in which it came is showing her wisdom, as she is filling that box with imagination rather than pressing buttons in response to some signals. It is unfortunate that play has lost respect in the world of early childhood in favor of electronic toys and computers, causing a notable decline in imagination.

Research also suggests that pretend play is an important facilitator of perspective taking, which is the ability to imagine the thoughts and perspective of others and to appreciate and take another's perspective. This is critically important for both language and social development.

Let me try to explain this connection to language. We first need to share attention before we can share meaning, the latter being my favorite definition of successful communication: my giving you a range of verbal and nonverbal cues so you can read my mind and understand what I'm thinking, that is, we share understanding and meaning (when that light bulb lights and you say, "Oh yeah, I understand!"). Joint attention also provides the earliest sense of other's having their own intentions, this ability to begin to appreciate another's perspective critical in communicating (the other person is having different thoughts then me and I need to understand those thoughts as well as share my own different thoughts). Symbol use means that you understand something stands for (represents) something else, which is what language is: the sound represents the thing.

Social competence is a rather complex idea involving a wide range of developmental and behavioral domains that has been defined as the skills and behaviors needed to succeed as a member of society. Among other things, it reflects the ability to take another's perspective, understanding that their perception and ideas differ from yours, a cornerstone of successful social interactions. These early social experiences provide a foundation upon which the skills for successful interactions with others are built.

As discussed above, I've heard many stories of young children engaging in a wide range of creative and often markedly annoying behaviors when reunited with a parent after a long day of work and preschool. Typically, this is an attempt to get the parent's attention and company. A solution to this nightly drama is to spend some quality time with your child when you reunite at the end of the day. You don't need to spend a lot of time (5 or 10 minutes can do it), the trick is to pay 100% attention to your child and to let them control the activity. If they want to play the same game with a superhero over and over until you want to scream, bear with them and give it (and them) your all. After those 5 or 10 minutes of unconditional and total attention, you can them take off your shoes, go to the bathroom, and make dinner. The quantity of time spent with your child is not nearly as important or impactful as the quality.

Chapter 11: Value Of Discipline As An Effective Parent

Discipline helps you to teach and guide your children about positive values and instills positive behaviors. An effective parenting model must use discipline proactively. The objective is to employ proactive tactics that encourage the sense of responsibility in your children, improve self-esteem, and enhance your relationship with your children. This entails setting limits, discerning between good and bad behaviors, discussing values and using distractions, time-outs, and logical consequences.

No single approach works best for all situations. For this reason, parents need to develop a range of skills and techniques such as:

Curbing annoying habits when applicable. Flag those behaviors that adversely impact your child, such as bad behavior, tantrums, and yelling. Don't ignore risky behaviors. Even though it's difficult to sit down and do nothing, the lack of attention deprives your child of the desired audience. However, please note that addressing annoying behaviors works when you notice and appreciate your child when she behaves well. Actions that you ignore will decrease while those you pay attention to will increase. When it comes to rewarding good behavior, create rules and expectations clearly. Appreciate your child when she follows the rules. For instance, when she picks up her toys, you can praise and then play some games with her.

When disciplining the child, ensure that you use logical consequences. For instance, take away the treats that relate to the child's bad behavior. If she misuses her toys, take them away for some time. Ensure the loss of privilege doesn't last too long since the child will concentrate on resentment, making it lose the lesson's intended meaning. If she colors the walls with crayons, make your child assist you with cleaning them and don't let her have the crayons for a while. You can also use a distraction for a child who starts to misbehave.

Showing your child the appropriate way to do various chores and behave is extremely important. Model for your child accordingly.

Use time-outs appropriately. A parent can use time-out to react to dangerous and negative behaviors like hitting, biting, and purposeful destruction. It's good to use time out when he or she concretely knows its meaning, usually at three years. Sit with the child in a place without distractions and try to explain one's mistakes and how to behave well next time. Once the time-out is complete, acknowledge when the child behaves well.

It's essential to continuously learn and practice effective parenting methods by using various discipline approach as your child grows. All discipline strategies should be age-appropriate to enable the child to differentiate between inappropriate and appropriate actions. Toddlers below 18 months won't understand these ideas yet.

Ensure your display of affection for your little one surpasses any punishes or consequences: kisses, hugs, and good-nurtured kinesthetic play are vital in reassuring your child that you love her. Attention and praise will motivate your child to follow the set rules. Instead of overloading your child with laws that may upset him or her, try to emphasize those meant for safety. Assist the child in complying with the rules by childproofing your house and getting rid of certain temptations.

In this post, we'll help you understand how to raise an emotional child and deal with tantrums in toddlers.

When Do Tantrums In children Start?

Children can start having tantrums as early as one year until age four. Nevertheless, the period where tantrums seem to be high is when the child is two or three years. Plus, tantrums that 2-year old displays will be different from that of a grown child since toddlers' challenges aren't' the same.

1. Causes of tantrums

When children fail to develop emotional regulation while growing, the causes of tantrums tend to vary. Note that there's no tantrum disorder, but they're more like a fever. They can be triggered by various problems that persist until you know what triggers them.

In most cases, the inability to control emotion is due to the underlying problem. Here are some of the typical causes of tantrums:

2. Environment

Tantrums can be caused by a child being overwhelmed by one's environment. For this reason, if your child tends to have tantrums regularly in specific surroundings, try to identify the triggers. This can be attributed to too many people, too much noise, excessive movements, distracting colors, or a massive size of the place.

3. Anxiety

Anxiety represents one of the greatest triggers of outbursts. While children don't typically experience full-grown anxiety, they'll still react to anxiety triggering conditions and melt-down when they feel stressed. Children who have learning disabilities or those who have gone through trauma or neglect might respond in this manner when they experience painful or uncomfortable circumstances.

4. Emotional control and ADHD

Some toddlers might experience more difficulties than others when dealing with emotions. They might be extremely passionate or impulsive. They might also have strong feelings than other children. For example, ADHD makes it difficult for toddlers to calm down, thus making their emotions escalate to anger or tantrums.

5. Difficulties in learning

When your child acts out frequently in school or when doing homework, it may indicate that he or she suffers from undiagnosed learning problem. He or she might have trouble with mathematics, so solving math tasks may make him irritable and frustrated. Instead of asking for assistance, he might shred the homework or begin to socialize with other children to form a diversion from the problem.

6. Irritability, depression, and autism

Irritability and depression occur in a subset of children with frequent and severe temper tantrums. The latest disorder, known as disruptive mood dysregulation disease (DMDD), manifests in children with severe outburst with chronic acute in between. Autism can also cause tantrums. Children with autism are susceptible to dramatic tantrums. These children are often rigid and highly dependent on repetition for their emotional comfort. For this reason, a slight change in the routine may upset them. Additionally, they might lack communication skills or language to explain their needs.

7. Sensory processing problems

In most cases, sensory processing issues are seen in autistic children, teens, and those children with ADHD. This problem might make a child overwhelmed in social settings and resort to tantrums.

Chapter 12: Academics And Sports

Academics play an important role in shaping the personality of a child. In addition to parents, a child has many teachers in their lives who teach them about the various subjects or English, mathematics, history, geography, etc. These individuals work to instill interest in learning, and in doing so help build a knowledge-base and understanding of various things surrounding children. However, just as academics are important for the mental development of a child, sports and extracurricular activities are equally important for the physical development of a child. Therefore, it is important for parents to teach their children how to achieve a balance between work and play, i.e. academics and sports.

If a child plays a sport through a school or community program, it has many benefits. If they constantly sit and stare at computer gadgets and textbooks and do not take a break, they won't be able to exercise their body and stay fit. However, if they participate in sports, they will be able to have a much needed break from technology and academics to work out, get their brain active again, and then return to their studies.

Just as sports help the child to focus on their academics, the latter also contributes in bringing a mental balance. If a child performs well academically, it will help them to increase their focus as part of a sports team and also help with logic and problem solving skills which they can utilize on the field. Moreover, if they do well academically, their chances will improve substantially in obtaining some type of financial assistance for post-secondary education.

Sports have a beneficial effect on a child's overall health: emotionally, physically and mentally. When children play a sport, they are providing themselves with a substantially healthy outlet that offers stress relief while doing something that they most likely enjoy. Regardless of the sport, it allows them to take their mind off term papers, other assignments, or grades. Though it may seem demanding at times with practice times and game schedules, involvement in a sport also provides them with the break that they need to help themselves not feel so bogged down.

This concept is something that many people do not quite understand, yet this is the reason why children are usually able to manage academics and sports fairly easily. The real job for a child is the academic part and the sport is their outlet, the much-needed break away from constant studies. So, it is important for children and their parents to realize the value of balancing academics and sports, as both are necessary.

Children have the natural tendency to be curious about many things and to explore different places, hence "play" acts as the medium that enables them to do so. Some of the elements of children's play are:

It is enjoyable and pleasurable

It is voluntary and spontaneous

It involves a make-believe element

It requires active engagement

It does not have any prescribed learning goals

Social Interaction

Social skills are very important for everyone. Parents should teach social skills to their children from an early age by encouraging them to meet new people and interact with them. This will help them to gain a new perspective of life and increase their confidence.

How many of us remember our first day at school, probably the first time when we were surrounded by so many unknown faces, without having those we were familiar with nearby? We may have been somewhat scared to leave our parents. This is because, before the first day of school, we are mostly limited to staying in our homes, interacting mostly with our family members, all the while being protected by them. Children are generally used to this protective shell and are thus typically unprepared to set foot out on their own without their parents' supervision.

Therefore, by teaching social skills and helping your children to meet new people, they will learn more about the world around them and how others think and act. If they have sufficient practice in this, they will understand that the world around them is an interesting, safe world. Thus, when they need to go places on their own (for e.g. on the first day of their school), they will not be as frightened.

However, social skills are not limited to having your children meet and interact with new people. There are numerous ways in which parents can help children to learn social skills and become social:

Encourage your child to be helpful; allow him to clear the dinner table or sort out the wash. Research has found that children who are a part of a culture which cares about people have higher chances of possessing better social skills.

Set a good example for them. Parents should be caring, respectful and polite towards each other if they wish their children to act in a similar way.

Even if it may seem difficult at times, show fondness to your children. When they are more affectionate and open, they are highly likely to have more friends.

Value the social skills your children already have. When they are polite or thoughtful, tell them about how proud you are of them. Expect, and also value mutual caring and respect.

Play down the competition level amongst your children. Be aware that each child is different and has different needs. Try to meet those needs.

Love uniquely. Children who are aware that they are being loved for themselves find it easier to share something about themselves with others.

Chapter 13: 5 Practical Tips To Managing Your Child's Screen Time

Responsible parenting help us parents avoid and prevent the many issues that can result from the usage of touchscreen devices and related innovations of technology. It is important to realize that any problem that arises from the use of these types of devices signals a problematic gap between the child and us the parents. As an adult, we must accept that it is always our fault or that we are always to be blamed in these situations. So, how can we stay updated to them using touchscreen devices and maintain the balance between its uses? How can we limit them from using the touchscreen device?

Sadly, not every problem can be resolved by encouraging parents to be more responsible because there are those bad parents who are extremely selfish and irresponsible in forcing their own flesh and blood for their own interest and security. A good example of this being child trafficking in which the child's own parent forces them to perform sexual acts for the cybersex illegal business.

But you can do your part by learning about the tips to be a responsible parent in relation with the use of technologies such as tablets, smartphones, mobile consoles, and other touchscreen devices.

Use it as Bonding Time

As a video gamer myself, I enjoy playing video games for entertainment. And as a parent, my daughter and I use the tablet for bonding time by playing video games and sometimes watching movies and listening music together. In these times I communicate with my child and explain concepts like how the game works and why she should do this or that. On the other hand, while watching movies, I enjoy asking my daughter questions like "Why did Dora do that?"; "Why is Pocoyo bad?" or "What did Barney mean by saying that?" It helps her understand, remain actively engaged, and her communication with me stays open.

In the case of an older child, my gamer friend and his 10-year-old son play an online game called **Summoners War: Sky Arena.** It is a monster-breeding game in IOS and Android. They bond and created a new hobby to enjoy which ultimately strengthened their relationship. Therefore, bonding time with children helps them to pick the right path usage of the touchscreen device. It leads children in proper understanding of the information encountered in game and other stuff offered by the device.

Set Rules for the Device

As I mentioned earlier, I myself was a video game addict when I was young. So, what helped me reduce the addiction toward video gaming? The rules and regulations my parents set to limit the use of the console. Same with touchscreen devices, setting rules and regulations free your children from becoming addicted by forcing them to allocate extra time on more important activities such as studying.

If you wondered what kinds of rule and regulations my parents specifically set for me, here it is: I was not allowed to play my console on a school day. I was only allowed to start playing my console from 9am to 6pm on Saturdays and 9am to 12pm on Sundays. If an examination was near, no console gaming for the whole week until the exam was finished or else the console would be hidden and locked for 2 months and I would receive a scolding. If I ever received a failure in my card class record, no video game for the rest of the school year. So summer break and Christmas break were the only vacation times that I could continuously play my console after doing my household tasks like bathing the dogs and assisting in cooking meals.

These rules and regulations forced me to study and prioritize the important things in life. It helped prevent me from destroying my life in my elementary and high school years which I have to give thanks to my parent for their concern towards me. For that reason, setting rules and regulations will not hurt the children emotionally or their feelings toward you, especially once they reach the point of living to earn money, they will appreciate and realize that it was in fact the right thing to do. Limiting them in the use of touchscreen devices such as tablets, PlayStation portable VITA, Nintendo 3 DS, and more will help them not to ruin their future life and health.

Use software for Security and Limitation

There are many software applications in the Worldwide Web which can help us parents to avoid our children from accessing the rated teen and adult video games, websites, movies, and music. Some of these applications are free and ready to download. Some are already conveniently bundled in the operation system for us. If you have knowledge in setting parental control in your operating system, it would be a great help.

Blocking websites that you think are bad for your children is another effective tool to stop them from accessing taboo websites. You can also use a plug-in into the browser that blocks websites that are rated for people of 18 years of age. You can also increase security to avoid the downloading of random software applications in the mobile and computer device. If you have sensitive and violent movies in your device, try placing it in a password protected folder.

In my case, you already know that my daughter knows how to turn on Wi-Fi and download games by herself in any Android device. But whenever I hand her the tablet, first I block the Mac address of the tablet from my router to prevent her from using the Internet. I do this to make sure that the tablet has no movies, which could potentially be inappropriate for her.

I have had an experience with her in which she was so afraid and cried loudly because of a TV show episode that she randomly opened. The episode that I forgot to delete was of The Walking Dead.

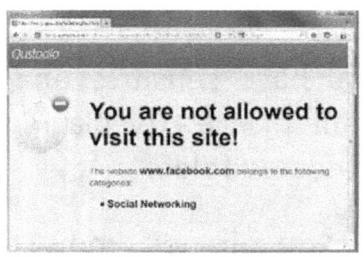

Qustodio, a free software for PC, Android, and iOS use for parental control, is a feature that monitors the online activities of the child. For example, tracking the web activity and blocking inappropriate content is one thing you can do. In addition to its services, you can also set rules for the use and access of the device. To unlock more tools, a premium subscription is required. Premium account additional features include a more robust toolset with location tracking, application controls, as well as call monitoring.

Give Them an Alternative Entertainment

As a child and a human being, they have the right to enjoy life. If you do not want to let them use touchscreen devices because you are afraid of the innovation of technology, give them an alternative entertainment. But, if I were you, do not let your children be ignorant in the innovation of technology because it is not avoidable. Did you ever see an office without a single computer? Or a supermarket without a point of sale system? So let them use it sometimes to learn and avoid being ignorant. Now, what are the alternative ways or things we could give to them?

a) Traditional Toys

At the age of 1 to 3 years old, toys like building blocks that are large enough for the child to not shallow are recommended. Musical instruments for toddlers like small drums could develop their creativity and love of music.

Children aged 4 to 12 years can already absorb information from you. Therefore, giving them sports instruments like balls and teaching them how to play with it is an alternative way of bonding without the use of touchscreen devices. Examples of sports you could teach your children are basketball and volleyball. Letting them play with relatives, friends, schoolmates and you helps build sportsmanship, learn teamwork, learn accepting failure and defeat, and helps enable them to socialize with people. In addition, board games like chess and scrabble increase their decision-making, logic, and for scrabble, spelling.

b) Pets

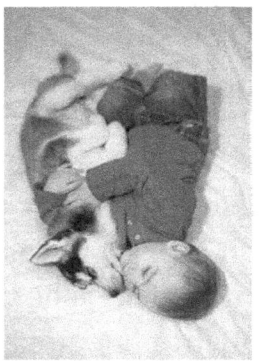

At the age of 3, children can already show signs of love and care to others. They also show signs of how to appreciate things and take responsibility. Pets like dogs and birds help children accelerate in the ability to give love, care, and show appreciation as well as responsibility. For example, my family also consists of our dog.

Our dog's name is Ice. He is a Husky breed. Huskies are loyal and friendly, especially to children. Huskies have rare cases of biting or barking at children. Huskies are energetic dogs which is why they love to play running games especially. Those are the reasons why my daughter loves to play with Ice.

Sometimes, Huskies are destructive because of stored energy, so sometimes I get angry and scold Ice. When I scold Ice, I can see my daughter's compassion to the dog shining through and sometimes she will even ask me why I am so angry with Ice. In that experience, I saw that children build emotional attachments to pets. The common emotion they feel is love and care.

The responsibility to pets appears in children after they have developed that emotional attachment with their pets. Children monitor pet's status. For example, my daughter monitors the level of water in Ice's drinking bucket. If the level of water is low, she adds water to it. Additionally, after she has eaten her meal, she volunteers to feed Ice. If Ice feels exhausted from the heat, she lets Ice enter the house and turns on the electric fan for Ice. Responsibility development and a reduction in obsession of gadgets is one of the many benefits we get from pets. It is very effective especially if exposed to pets at a very young age.

Get Outdoors

Connecting with nature or society, for all children in any age, gives many benefits in the growth and development of children. Nature gives children fresh air to breath, sunshine that helps provide Vitamin D which is essential for growth and seeing the actual appearance of objects that they might have seen on the touchscreen device, such as animals and plants. Letting them socialize with other people helps build their social behavior and development. Getting outdoors like playing tag, or going to the beach to swim, helps them exercise their body to develop their physical strength and endurance and increases their energy storage. Alternative activities, similar to joining a church singing choir, help them develop spiritual relationship with the Divine.

And the final tip of this chapter that will help parents monitor their children's touchscreen device usage is:

Be a Role Model and a Good Teacher

Children are not dumb as some may think they are. I personally feel that all those individuals who believe children are dumb are they themselves dumb for even thinking that. Children are simply lacking experience in the real world, but they are most definitely not dumb. Setting rules and regulations and saying "No you cannot do that," when yourself are always doing that act and disobeying that rule not only makes you a hypocrite. Children learn things and follow what adults do through observation and modeling, especially if you are the parent of that child.

If you tell them to stop playing with the tablet while you are obsessively playing **Clash of Clan** on your iPad or Android tablet, they will be confused and wonder why they need to stop if you as an adult constantly use it. This is a case of irresponsible parenting. Think first before giving them an order, or try to explain it to them like as a teacher would do.

In my work, I need to face the computer monitor to do my work. While my daughter loves watching movies like **Pocoyo**, **Dora**, or **Barney**, we share the one monitor for both of our needs. Half of the monitor screen is dedicated to my work while the other half is used for her movies.

When I ask her to stop because it is time for her afternoon nap, I explain to her how important it is for her and her growth. At times, she will even ask me why I don't stop looking at the monitor if she needs to stop watching cartoons. I always say that I need to do this because it is my work and how it is important as it allows us to buy the milk that you drink and the food that you eat. And the same technique applies here as with the tablet, you need to stop at times because you are tired and you need to place the device within a reasonable distance from your eyes so that they will not hurt.

Being a good role model and providing a simple but thorough explanation will greatly benefit your child. In the process, they will learn that it is bad for them to disobey you and they will also learn the reasons behind many concepts through simple explanations that help them learn the cause and consequence of certain acts. If your child is between the ages of 9 to 12, it is probably more effective to be a little more realistic by providing even realistic and scary consequences like "If you do not want to be a homeless person when you grow up as an adult, learn to prioritize your studies and your education." Explaining concepts is always the best method because in this manner the child will lean exactly what it is they are doing right or wrong and why, but if explanations and scolding them do not work, you can then resort to spanking the child if you are in a country in which spanking or minimally creating pain in a children for disciplinary purposes is legal, such as in Asian countries.

 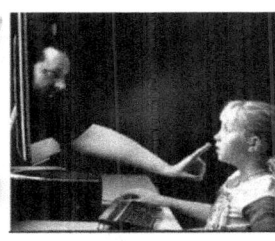

Deleting files rated as adults only is also considered being a good role model. For instance, a 12-year-old boy who is entering the puberty stage is beginning to fantasize about sexual encounters, an example is wet dreams; they might look into these acts on the Internet and then learn to watch pornographic material for his sexual pleasure. In particular, if you as a father are storing pornographic material on your tablet or smartphone memory and your child accidentally accesses it, this will increase his confidence in watching pornographic material because he will think it is morally right since his father is also viewing the material.

To keep them away and secure from offline and online predators, teach your children to avoid strangers and to avoid receiving gifts from unknown people or even authorities. Help them understand and answer any question they may have as best you can so they will be aware and not easily give their trust to other people, especially in adults that are not blood related. Teach them to never post vital information to the Worldwide Web, such as their home address, contact number, and parent and family names. And most importantly, teach them to never post family problems on social networking sites or chat rooms to avoid being lured in by predators who may pose as being concerned.

Chapter 14: Why Sibling Rivalry Happens: The Main Causes

The causes of sibling rivalry are as many as they are varied. While we will discuss most of these shortly, many experts postulate that sibling rivalry breeds from competition and jealousy, which can then escalate into fights and arguments.

The other factors that can cause sibling rivalry include:

Changing Needs

As your children grow, mature, and learn more about themselves and the world they live in, their needs, fears, and identities will change; so will how they relate with each other.

A great example is how because of the natural need to have a sense of ownership, toddlers will want to protect their toys and belongings. Because of this, older kids are likely to react in a negative manner or aggressively when a younger child grabs their toys and personal belongings.

Different Personalities

Your individual children have individual temperaments; they have different moods, adaptability, and character. This individuality plays a role in how a child reacts to changes in his or her environment. A child that is quick to upset may fail to get on with one that likes to kid around a lot. We can say the same for children who are in constant need of a parent's guidance and comfort; rivalry may develop when the other children feel they are getting the short end of the stick.

Disability/Sickness

Most children do not understand the needs of a disabled or sick child. They may translate the fact that you spend more time caring for the sick or disabled child as proof that you love the child more, which may cause jealousy, competition, and trivial arguments bred out of resentment.

Your Role

Children learn how to handle most things from the people in their lives, their role models. If you and your partner do not have a healthy way of resolving disagreements and problems, it will reflect in your children's' behavior. For instance, if you and your spouse resolve problems in an aggressive, nonproductive manner, your children will learn this and use it to solve their arguments.

On the other hand, if your children see you handle problems in a safe, loving, and respectful manner, they will learn to do the same with each other.

Age Differences

Age differences is one of the most common cause of sibling rivalry especially considering that children of different ages have specific in-built needs.

Most conventional families try to create a gap of 4-5 years between children as a way to enhance independence and understanding in a child before adding another member to the family. While this is great, it can cause rivalry between children especially when you fail to foster understanding in the older child who has more independence and varying priorities.

The clash in mindset will lead to rivalry especially when the older child does not understand the needs of the younger child and the need to be patient and kind as the younger child grows and matures.

The above are the main causes of sibling rivalry. Now that we understand them, we are going to outline specific strategies you can use to end sibling rivalry and help your children develop better relationships.

Chapter 15: The 11 Commandments Of Toddler Discipline

Disciplining an elementary school kid is very different from when you try to do the same for a toddler. The older kid understands language and they know the rules. They know that mummy or daddy said we should not touch the TV because it may fall and break and that means we shall have nowhere to watch cartoons. A toddler wonders why they cannot touch that beautiful screen and probably thinks that you are being mean – or that they are being kept from the fun stuff.

Does it mean that you let them off the hook probably because you think that they are too young to understand rules and consequences? Absolutely not! You want to bring up a good world citizen and member of your family don't you? Then do not spare that toddler; teach them to do right.

However:

Discipline for a toddler is quite a touchy issue and every parent who has succeeded in raising well mannered and intelligent children has had to learn the following commandments – mostly the hard way. In the practical ways to deal with behavior and emotional challenges in the previous chapter, you will notice that the solutions to these issues rely on the commandments discussed below. Observe them as you discipline your child and you are likely to have an easy time and successfully achieve the desired results

Statements must be short and sweet

Their little minds cannot comprehend long sentences. For this reason, you find that they only understand short statements. For instance, they will understand "come here", "no biting", "stop", "no", "no touching".

However, if you go for "Liam, you know it's not good to bite your friends" or "Mandy, you need to stop pulling on the cable". Trust me; you will lose Liam right after "you know" and Mandy at "you need". Just say "Liam, no biting", or "Mandy, stop pulling".

Please, no yelling

The loudest voice you can use may stop your child from doing whatever – or not especially when it becomes a habit. However, it signals that you are losing control – of yourself and the situation and your lovely child may get scared of your voice but they are not going to respect.

All of us yell at times but you realize that at those moments, you are not feeling in control – and that little one notices it too. Do not be surprised when they assume your instruction when you yell.

Do not yell. What you do, is to change your voice. Understand that it's not the volume, but the tone of your voice that communicates and gets the points across. Remember how that soft spoken teacher was the most respected – and most strict? You probably had a funny name for the yelling one you never listened to – you do not want to be this one.

Therefore, you may want to focus more on tone and keep your volume normal when giving instruction to a toddler.

Act immediately – on the spot

They do not have a long term memory to remember what they did and also they do not have the mental capacity to connect previous action and present consequences.

If your child is doing something wrong, you should never postpone serving the consequences. If they need to be disciplined, it has to be done right on the spot of action. Do not wait because five minutes later, she/he will be onto something else and they won't remember what wrong they did to deserve punishment.

Do not make promises as 'pay' for good behavior

"If you eat your food, ill buy you chocolate", "if you are nice to your friends, I'll get you that toy you want" it works, doesn't? They will do what you want to get that reward —no arguments or rebellion. Phew!

It's easy and that's why it's very tempting. Do not do it. It's true you will get them to behave, especially when you offer something they love. However, what you will have succeeded to do is to bring up a two or three year old who knows that any good behavior has a price tag. You do not want your child to turn out manipulative or corrupt, do you?

Choose what battles are worth fighting

You do not want to fight with your child every time over every little thing they do. They will assume that you are always fighting or saying "no" and won't pay attention to your correction. For instance, if you say "don't touch" 25 times a day, eventually, it will lose its effectiveness – and they will touch.

Therefore, pick your battles. Have behaviors you cannot condone and those that are too insignificant to bother with.

For instance, if they scream every time you pick a call, just ignore them. Eventually, they will know that they will not get a reaction out of you and drop the behavior.

Condemn the behavior, not the child

You love your child, don't you? You want to raise a child who knows that their parent loves them. However, we sometimes jeopardize this when we start to condemn our children when they behave badly, instead of focusing only on the behavior.

Always tell them that a particular behavior s bad; never tell them that they are bad. Tell them that what they did was foolish, but do not tell them that they are foolish. This is the best way to communicate "I love you, but I do not love the way you are acting right now" or "you are smart but what you are dong isn't that smart".

Correct, redirect, repeat

When with a toddler around the house, you'll probably do this all day. You will catch them doing something they shouldn't, tell them "no" and attempt to distract them with a different activity. Chances are, they will try to go back to the previous "wrong activity", which they find to be entertaining for some reason and see if they can get away with it.

It can be frustrating, but if you want to etch the "I should not do this" memory in their little brain, you should not give up. Correct, redirect and repeat even if they have returned to that activity for the tenth time.

There shall be consequences for actions

Teach your child that there are outcomes for their behavior. It is important for them to understand that actions come with consequences — a lesson that will be of great help in their adult life.

Some consequences include missing out on activities they love, the time-out corner and so on. For instance, if they bite or hit their friends while playing, they ought to know that it will automatically earn them some time in the time-out corner, alone and with no one to play with.

Note: missing out on your love should never be a consequence. Do not push them away or refuse to cuddle, comfort or be there for them when they genuinely need you as punishment.

You shall not back down or compromise to avoid conflict

Sometimes it's tempting to let them have their way, especially when they roll, scream and kick in a public place and everyone is giving you the "give them what they want so they can shut up" look.

If you want to reinforce or discourage certain behavior, you will need to be consistent in the direction you give your child. There shouldn't be times you allow them to do something you do not want them doing just to prevent a meltdown. For instance, if you said they cannot have candy, stick to your guns even when in a supermarket and they are standing right in front of it screaming their lungs out.

You see, the message you want to send them is "you cannot have candy" not "you cannot have candy, but you can grab all you want if you scream loud enough". Remember, toddlers are experts at studying your game and they will know what drives you to give in - they will do it all the time.

Always give them choices

Make your child to feel important and in control by giving them a chance to choose. You do not want to raise a child, who knows only to be dominated, never being able to make their choices, do you?

However, there shouldn't be many options to choose from, as this may confuse the child. Also, they should include the things you want to accomplish. For instance say "It's your choice: You can put on that dress or this one."

Be a reflection of what you want to see with your child.

Kids do not do what they are instructed to do. They are most likely to learn their behavior and communication skills from their environment. You are their first contact with the world and therefore, they will learn from you. That kid you think to be too little to see and understand is observing your every move. They are learning how to handle situations and how to talk by watching you.

Therefore, you have to model the values you want your child to adopt. If you do not want them to talk back, don't talk back to other adults or them, if you don't want them to complain, stop complaining about the weather or the electricity. Do not tell them what you want them to do or become, show them.

Chapter 16: The Absent Parent – How To Diffuse The Tension

As a single parent, your most important job is to help your child cope and deal with the absence of the lost parent. There can be plenty of reasons for the absence of a parent; divorce or untimely death of your spouse or other circumstances. Either way, you must make sure that you have dealt with your own feelings about the past relationship. Be capable of talking about it freely without letting your emotions cloud your judgment.

Your child may want to discuss the absence of a parent.

If you are unwilling to answer, then he/she would seek answers from elsewhere. This may result in the child not getting accurate information about your family situation.

On the other hand, if you do answer his/her questions, it will only strengthen your relationship. They will also learn to trust you and rely on you in delicate matters.

The first question that you may be asked is, 'Do I have a dad?'

As children come in contact with other kids who have both parents, they start wondering about the existence of their own missing parent. You must answer this question without making a fuss out of it.

The answer to the question 'where is my dad' must be answered in simple non-vague terms.

You must not confuse your kid, so be transparent about this question. If you don't know where the other parent is then simply say that, instead of making up a story and lying to them. Sometimes children just need the information to answer the questions of other children. If they don't have the answer to vital questions, then the topic becomes a very sensitive issue for them. They become vulnerable and prone to bullying or teasing.

The next question that you can be asked is 'if the absent parent loves the child or not?'

While answering this question try to be as positive as you can. Answers like 'I am sure if they knew you, they would love you just like me' can be good for the child as they like being loved.

If your child asks why the absent parent is not living with you both, then try to explain to your child that not all families have both the parents. Reassure them that they are a part of a complete family. They should feel loved and accepted and be proud of the family they have.

Providing basic information about the missing parent: If your child asks for information like the name of the missing parent, what they looked like, etc. then provide the information as best you can. Let them create their own identify of the absent parent.

Finally one of the most important questions that you'll have to answer is, if your child can meet the absent parent.

If you can arrange a meeting and are comfortable doing so, then go ahead. The relationship between your ex partner and the child may (will) be different from your relationship with them. It would not benefit the child, if you try to prevent the child from meeting their father, using your experience with him.

If you are not in contact with the absent parent then you must tell your child that at that moment they can't meet the other parent. There is no point in creating false hope.

The key to enable your child to live in a healthy and balanced atmosphere as a single parent is communication.

You must ensure that your child does not feel uncomfortable discussing anything with you. You must develop a routine to provide your child with a sense of security and make time to reinforce an emotional connection.

As a single parent, you must seek and accept support. You need to build a network of people whom your child is comfortable with and who can help you around the household. Cultivate independence in your child. Show your love to the child, give him/her the unconditional love and support that he/she requires. At the same time, be careful not to spoil your child and remember to set limits.

Being a single parent is tough for both you and the child, but together and with a little positivity, you both can easily cope with it.

Chapter 17: Parenting Skills

Despite your individual opinions, fathers and mothers play an equal role in their children's lives when it comes to their physical, emotional and financial well being. Studies show that children who are well fathered end up being more confident, are more likely be academically successful and have greater self control. However, some fathers, especially those who were raised by single mothers may not know what it takes to be a good father. While every father is different in his own way, there are some fundamental skills that they can acquire to become effective parents. As a father, whether you realize it or not, you are a role model to your child. As such, you are supposed to be a positive role model through your actions in order to show your child how to be honest, respectful and humble. Establish high moral standards and treat other people exactly how you would want to be treated. Own up to your mistakes when you have wronged, and do not be hesitant to say you are sorry. Be mindful of your behavior, and always assume that your child is watching you. Make sure your habits, actions and words are something you would want your child to copy. While it is important to discipline your child, perhaps the best approach would not be to shout, pound on tables and ridicule them as this can damage their self esteem. Establish realistic limits and enforce your authority in a calm and fair manner. This will go a long way in reassuring your child that you love him and reduce the chance of him/her losing their respect for you.

On the other hand, taking some time out to spend with your child can make them feel loved and important, which will support their psychological and emotional well being. The added benefit is that you will have an opportunity to bond with your child and learn about his vices, values, aspirations and fears. Engage him in physical activities like sports, as well as intellectual activities like reading. Do not forget to also engage in productive tasks such as cleaning the yard and grocery shopping that will teach responsibility.

The way the dad and mom treat each other in front of the kids will also play a role in setting an example for the children. It is therefore important for the both of you to treat each other with consideration and respect, whether married or otherwise. If your child notices you treating the mom with respect, he is more likely to treat his future spouse the same way. Avoid attacking the personality of your child's mother, or in that case, incline him/her to take your side in case of a conflict.

Since the beginning of time, there has always been plenty of over parenting and one-upmanship, and who is more important than the other. While women seem to have won the battle hands down, this has turned out to be a complete disaster for the countless children out there who as a result, grow up in broken and fatherless homes. On their parts, fathers have come out to dispute statistics. In part, you will find that children who grow up with their fathers end up doing better than their counterparts who are raised by single mothers. However, it is important to note that both fathers and mothers are equally important, and complimentary.

The problem in modern families is that the father's role in parenthood has been overlooked and replaced with the assumption that children are better off with the mother's maternal provision. In part, women are also right in some way. Men cannot make second mothers; in fact, they only end up being inferior mothers. While fathers can care for small children and infants in a pinch, they are not very well suited for it. You can compare mothering to a man fixing a car, which simply means it is a forced task. A man will feel very tender towards his child; he will become protective of him and will go to work with its safety in mind. However, rarely will he understand the child's vocalizations in the same way as a woman, nor the nonverbal communication and nursing of the baby. In addition, he will usually be clumsier when it comes to cleaning, feeding and dressing the child. On their part, infants and small children usually have a standard emotional communication. Since women tend to think more on an emotional level than men, this comes as an advantage to them. However, make no mistake, just because men do not make very effective mothers does not mean they do not have a role to play. In truth, the fact that fathers are not mothers makes them important to their children.

As your child grows, he or she must learn to communicate directly, think rationally and navigate the physical world. Humans, in general, need to learn these things, since we are cultural beings. While nobody has to teach a baby how to suckle or even cry, as they grow, the number of things that they need to learn also grows exponentially. It therefore becomes our responsibility to teach them. While emotional support and encouragement may be helpful, deliberate and rational teaching is very different from caring for a baby. For example, when teaching your child how to ride a bike, you need to involve encouragement, but more importantly, instruction. The same goes for learning how to drive. While you may take these things for granted now, they were once equally relevant challenges to you once. If you were not taught by your father, it was another man in your life.

Another important role dads play in their children's development is setting a good behavioral example. There is nothing more pathetic than a young man who turns to emotional response when faced with a problem. Physical and temper tantrums may be the norms for small children, but when it comes to an adolescent, this may be asking for prison time. Since mothers relate to toddlers and small children emotionally, it sets a pattern for life. While this emotional bond is crucial to the infant's well being and to ensuring an emotionally functional human being, if it is not balanced with a different kind of relationship, it can obscure maturity. Now, this is where fathers come into play. They provide a refuge from the emotionally taxing and demanding relationship between the mother and the child. This becomes indispensable as the child develops, approaches maturity and starts to take steps towards independence. Obviously this is also good for mothers. If there is no father figure to provide an emotional time out, chances are the moms will exhaust themselves as they try to manage their teenagers with similar techniques they applied when they were younger. Since a mother and her child have a strong psychological bond, it is no wonder that people are inclined to perceive mothers as the default parents. This sense of sentimentality has gone a long way into influencing democratic decision making.

This is nothing new, and you can see common examples throughout the world. Catholics for instance, venerate Mary, the mother of Jesus, the Chinese character of good, known as hao, is represented by an ideogram of a mother and a child, while Buddhist on the other hand iconize Kuan Yin. As you can see, it would be a futile effort to try and eliminate or replace the mother figure in the average mind, as it seems to be directly associated with our most basic ideology of parenthood and everything good in the world. The question we are left to find an answer to is what you can you do to restore the recognition, importance and respect of fatherhood? Certainly we cannot achieve this if we claim that there is no significant difference between fathers and mothers, since that would be a false and deceptive argument. Although it may seem like self-contradictory, the best way to achieve this is to put emphasis on the difference between fathers and mothers. Rather than emphasizing on the ideal that fathers should be second mothers, we need to acknowledge the importance to children of fathers being men, and then provide them with the needs that mothers cannot.

Chapter 18: On Parent-Connectedness And Entering His World

RULE # 10 – Keep Your Child Connected

Always make sure to spend time with your children. As most parents already know, you are the key to his happiness and success. A child, even with a single Mom or Dad raising him, would find it excited to go home after school and have dinner together if what he will go home to is a parent who cares and takes care of his every need. Truth is, what a child wants is to spend time with his parent. Think of yourself as your child's base camp. Isn't it comforting to know that after a whole day of being busy and not being together, your child finds solace in you? Your child needs a place to stop, to settle in, and to remember that fun and relaxation time always happens at home.

For a busy sole parent who is always required to do things outside the house, here are some helpful tips:

Take your child with you even if it is about work. You sure will have considerate bosses especially if they are aware of your situation.

During days off from work, bring him to a museum, go for a bike around the park, or go see a movie together. This will help you know your child's interests and be able to open up and share things and experiences with your child.

Real connection and live presence spent with your children cannot be substituted by fancy gadgets and modern technology. What is good with real connectedness is the continuous flow of conversation. Since most parents today are competing with e-conversations and messaging, make sure that you steal your child away from these gadgets as often as you can especially during stages when you can easily control him. Show your child that you are a better communicator than cellphones, chatrooms, and emails.

RULE # 11 – Let Yourself into Your Child's World

Being a single parent is not easy. Every day, there will be different challenges and roadblocks. Most of which will come from the kind of environment and culture he is born rather than from anything you have done as a parent. So be prepared. After the toddler years, your child will enter school and this will take up most of his time. Oftentimes, this will pull him away from you. Of course, your child going to school is not a bad idea, but you must accept the fact that you do not have total control of what happens at school. Some experiences may work against your relationship with your child, while some may not. He will eventually encounter bullies at school or hear derogatory remarks from mean people. He will soon be embarrassed or humiliated because of the situation of his family. His friends might try to pull him away from you. Accept that this is really the reality of life.

So what's a single parent do? A lot. You may not be able to challenge the twenty first century culture or reform school curricula but you can always set a good example to your child. The leadership and guidance you have given from his early years, if done right and consistently applied in the house will help him be on track, or at least put him back on it. Remember, you are the most influential person in his life. He takes cues on you and you will always be his parent. So even if you think your child has gone too far from you, go find him. It does not matter how you do it or how he will react. What matters is he is still your child, and you his Mom/Dad.

Chapter 19: Awareness Of Logical Consequences

Teaching your child about consequences is an effective way to develop his sense of responsibility and become accountable for his actions. In effect, he chooses the consequence, he experiences. Whatever his age, it is necessary to be consistent in disciplining him, stick to the rules you set, and enforce the consequence of every misbehavior.

A. Logical Consequences vs. Natural Consequences

There are two common forms of consequences- logical and natural.

Natural consequences refer to the inevitable outcome of his action. For instance, your child does not want to wear a jacket. While on the outside, he feels cold and uncomfortable, but he has no jacket to warm himself. It is the consequence of his choice not to bring his jacket. He cannot blame others for his misery because it is his choice. The learning experience teaches him a lesson to always bring a jacket.

Logical consequences are basically the result of your child's irrational acts that may endanger his safety or life. They are formulated to keep him away from hard and require adult intervention to be enforced. When devising them, it is important that they must not affect the mutual respect between the parent and the child. Logical consequences must be problem-related and reasonable.

B. The 3 R's and H of Logical Consequences

This simple formula identifies the four major criteria that you need to observe to ensure that the logical consequences are solutions to inappropriate behavior and are not forms of punishments.

Related. The consequence is related to behavior.

Respectful. It is firmly and kindly enforced to the child, avoiding shame, pain, or blame. The consequence should be respectful to those involved.

Reasonable. The consequence is seen by the child and by the parent as within the bounds of reason.

Helpful. It helps to correct misbehavior without inflicting any pain.

For example, the child spills his milk. The related consequence is to make him clean it up. A respectful remark is, "What do you need to do now?" It is reasonable to let him clean up the mess. It will be helpful if you will show him how to do it but do not do it for him.

Remember that, if one of the criteria is missing, the consequence is not logical anymore.

C. The 4Rs of Punishment

Eliminating one of the positive criteria of logical consequences will result in negative responses that are embodied in the 4Rs, making the child resent the person who is disciplining him and feel bad.

Resentment.

"It is unfair." "I cannot trust adults."

Revenge.

"I will get even."

Rebellion.

"I will show them that I can do whatever I want."

Retreat (or sneakiness).

"I will not let them catch me next time."

Are they effective?

Both are effective strategies because of the following:

It allows the child to make a choice.

It is closely-tied to the kid's behavior, giving him lessons when he misbehaves.

It is concerned with both present and future behavior, training the child to become responsible for his actions.

It does not punish or shame the child, keeping the deed separated from the doer.

It is done in a calm environment, making him feel secure and safe.

To ensure its effectiveness, you must think ahead and prepare a proper response. You should avoid "saving" your child and refrain from stepping in. Allowing him to experience the consequence will teach him vital lessons. If the consequence does not work during the first enforcement, keep putting it into action until it resolves the problem.

Helpful tips to effectively use Natural and Logical consequences:

Identifying the reasons.

For every action, there is a reason. Same goes when your child misbehaves. It is possible that he wants to get your complete attention, get even, gain control or power, or feel inadequate.

Paying no attention is one classic example of getting attention, and gaining power over adults. Say, your child is playing and you give him 5 minutes to finish and put his toy away. Even if you say "one-minute left," he keeps on playing and having fun. Now, all your attention is on him.

Deciding whose problem it is.

Let your child faces his own problem. Do not interfere, as long as the consequences will not harm his safety or health.

If it begins to rain and your kid does not heed your warning that playtime is up, he might get drenched. This is a natural consequence.

If he does not put the toys away, it can be your problem because leaving them outside is not safe because someone might get it if. If you are training him to become more responsible by bringing back his toys inside your house, and he refuses to do it, you can use a logical consequence.

3. Offering choices or alternatives.

Keep in mind that logical consequence is the result of your child's choice. Offer safe, positive, and limited choices that will prompt him to behave accordingly or do something about the problem.

Tell your kid, "You need to pick your toys now. If you leave them outside, you are not allowed to play them tomorrow. It's your choice."

4. Being firm.

After he makes a choice, you need to follow through the consequence. Do not waver, show him that you are serious about enforcing the rule. If you slip even once, the child knows that he can get past the logical consequence and will attempt to do it again.

Say, **"All right then, I can see that you do not want to play with your toys tomorrow."**
Pick up the toys and store them away, where he cannot reach them. Most probably, your child will cry and throw fits, just be calm, and remind him that he already made a choice.

5. Talking about choices in a positive way.

Giving choices is more appealing to your children compared to a warning. Though the logical consequence may be similar, by being positive instead of threatening, you prevent power struggles.

Maybe if you rephrase your words, he will show cooperation. "I want you to play with your toys tomorrow, so let's pick them up and bring inside, so they will not disappear like your favorite ball which you left it here."

6. Letting the child know if he had done something good.

As soon as you see your child correcting his behavior and doing what is appropriate, acknowledge it. Avoid over-praising, simply say it's great. It will reinforce his motivation to meet your expectations and follow the rules.

If the next day, you see your child picking up his toys and putting them in proper storage even if you do not remind him, say

"Wow, I can see that you are taking care of your toys. I am proud of you!"

7. Involving your child when deciding on the consequences.

Because it primarily involves the child, and he is the one who will suffer the consequences of his behavior and choices, ask suggestions from him.

Initiate a conversation with your child and discuss what will happen if he does not bring in the toys after playing. He will probably say that other children might get them. Then, you can say that toys cost money and if they are lost, it would not be possible to buy toys for him. Maybe he would answer that he might be able to help you buy new toys because he has savings. In the end, you both agreed that the best solution is for him to pick them up after playing in the outdoors.

When imposing logical consequences to young children (8 years old and below), remember the following:

Calm down. Step back for a while, take a deep breath, and control impulses to yell or punish the child.

Don't be a bully. Rein your anger because it carries a threat of violence to a child, like the monsters in fairy tales.

Stay connected and present. Do not leave him alone when he is misbehaving. Timeouts may be useful for some time, but it is important for the child not to be left alone for long, or he will feel neglected during times that he is out of control. Wait for him to calm down.

Look for appropriate logical consequence. Use a consequence that is age-appropriate and will make him feel valued, listened to, understood, and respected.

Be private. Always deal with the situation privately. Avoid embarrassing your child by publicly punishing or correcting him.

Move on. After the consequence is over or the time for it has been served, refrain from asking more apologies or lecturing about the behavior. You may gently ask him what he learns from the experience and then allows him to go back to his routine, hoping in your heart that he learned a lesson and will not repeat the act.

Chapter 20: Don'ts Of Being A Conscious Parent

o Don't set unreasonable and impractical opinions. It would never boost up child's natural interest and instincts.

o Don't allow them to eat out or in seclusion. Eat meals together as a family to the maximum. If all meals cannot be met, at least one meal with the family is a must.

o Don't allow your kid to skip their normal sleeping routine. Natural and sufficient sleep will keep your child happy and healthy.

o Don't discourage free play and adventure as they contribute towards building neural tracks inside child's brain.

o Don't overprotect them and mistakes and painful experiences are akin to building blocks of mind and body. Allow them to have their way but be there to support them as and when needed.

o Don't aspire to remove all stumbling blocks from your child's path. No parent can ensure that. Instead, prepare him to face and overcome those, if any.

o Don't over-schedule your child with innumerable activities. He isn't a robot! Let him make his own healthy choices.

o Don't even over-instruct your child. There is great learning hidden in trial-and-error method.

o Don't blame your child. Remember, that at this juncture of his life you are his guide. If he has committed some mistake, may be you are somewhere responsible for that.

o Don't get into habit of resolving problems and issue for your child. Let him do it on his own. And don't render even uncalled advice.

o Don't stress that only you know the right way to do things. You never know, your child may suggest some smarter solution. Encourage them to find alternative solutions.

o Don't out rightly dismiss your kid's ideas. Encourage them to brainstorm.

o Don't break your promises and strive hard to keep commitments. This is going to teach them to do same.

o Don't act like a ring leader or the "Master".Your child is not your obedient pet or slave. Allow him to bloom into an independent and acreative individual.

o Don't justify any improper action or behavior of yours. You ought to keep your morals and ethics above convenience.

o Don't pretend that you are Mr. or Ms. Know-all. No one is. Being unsure is being utterly human.

o Don't be phony, cheat or a liar. Your truthfulness and honesty will set him on the right path.

o Don't thrust arbitrary power on your child. Teach him that power always accompanies responsibility.

o Don't deride anyone in front of your child. Treat everyone with value and respect.

Chapter 21: Enjoying Your Teenagers

Teenage years mean that you only have a couple of years left to be with your children on a full-time basis. They will be graduating, working, moving out, and marrying soon enough. Have a great time with your teenager now. As a parent, you should take the initiative to make the remaining years together memorable and special.

Let daily encounters be a time to share and communicate. Asking how their day went is safe, and a great way to have a more detailed discussion. It will also convey the message that you care about what you teen is doing throughout the day. It's als a way to stay updated on what's new or what is needed by your child. You can also share how your day went, allowing them to know you more and see your world.

Working together side by side will not only make great memories, but it is also a great training opportunity for your teen. Why not wash dishes together? You could make it a fun chore at the same time. Plus you are teaching your teen to become a more responsible person when you assign him or her a task. Or you could do gardening together. Involving your teens in the responsibilities at home will not only prepare them to be future responsible adults, but will also make them more committed to the family. Give them responsibilities appropriate to their age.

Create unique ways of spending time together. Put your creative juices to work. Sit down together and make a plan for how you will spend your Saturdays. Set aside time just for you and your teen.

Involve your teens in the planning of the family's annual vacation. Let your teen have a say on some of the family activities. You will find out once again how fun it is to spend time with your teens. Their world may be different from yours, but it is also enjoyable. Your teenager is still the best gift in the world!

Conclusion

Every generation has something to add to the evolution of parenting, and all of them only want one thing – the best for their children without having to please them.

Remember, history has a way of repeating itself, and at some point, it does pay to look back in time for guidance which will help your children understand things better for them to be able to raise their own children. Every experience leaves an impact on children.

Technology is a double edged sword. As a modern day Supermom, you need to use technology to raise healthy, happy and well-behaved children. This is more about striking a balance between the battle for supremacy between gadgets and your child. After all it is for your child's safety and wellbeing.

You will find advantages as well in raising a tech-savvy kid, but it need not always mean you need to hand over or buy them fancy gadgets for them to learn. Setting rules is not the only thing you need to do as a parent, you also need to be aware of the latest in technology and be cautious about bullying and any personal data being shared if your gadget is being used by your children.

It is a Pandora's box, and if you are not willing to spend the time to learn about how you can keep your child safe from monsters lurking online, avoid getting your child anywhere close to a gadget or the internet.

As a parent, it is our responsibility to help our child survive the changing times, while we are on the same learning path ourselves.

Good Luck on your turning into a gadget-free Supermom. And always remember, old is gold, but the new is not all that bad too!

www.ingramcontent.com/pod-product-compliance
Lightning Source LLC
Chambersburg PA
CBHW072006070526
44583CB00015B/1357